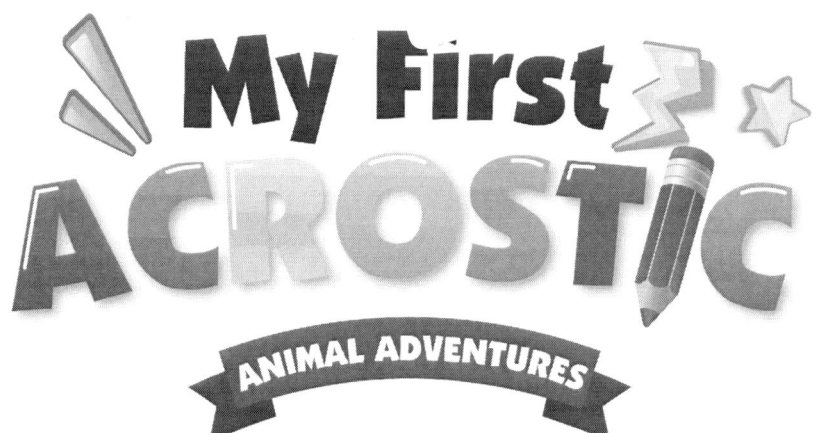

Future Voices

Edited By Vicky Hackney-Williams

First published in Great Britain in 2020 by:

Young Writers
Remus House
Coltsfoot Drive
Peterborough
PE2 9BF
Telephone: 01733 890066
Website: www.youngwriters.co.uk

All Rights Reserved
Book Design by Ashley Janson
© Copyright Contributors 2020
Softback ISBN 978-1-83928-922-4

Printed and bound in the UK by BookPrintingUK
Website: www.bookprintinguk.com
YB0441T

Welcome to a fun-filled book of acrostic poems!

Here at Young Writers, we are delighted to introduce our new poetry competition for KS1 pupils, *My First Acrostic: Animal Adventures*. Acrostic poems are an enjoyable way to introduce pupils to the world of poetry and allow the young writer to open their imagination to a range of topics of their choice. The colourful and engaging entry forms allowed even the youngest (or most reluctant) of pupils to create a poem using the acrostic technique and with that, encouraged them to include other literary techniques such as similes and description. Here at Young Writers we are passionate about introducing the love and art of creative writing to the next generation and we love being a part of their journey.

From the jungle to the ocean, pets to mythical monsters, these pupils take you on a journey through the animal kingdom and showcase their budding creativity along the way. So we invite you to dive into these pages and take a glimpse into these blossoming young writers' minds. We hope you will relish these roarsome poems as much as we have.

Contents

Gaelscoil Éadain Mhóir, Brandywell

Fiadhna O'Neill (7)	1
Mia Pirone (8)	2
Dearbhla Devine (7)	3
Cayden Williams (7)	4
Caislín Clarke (8)	5
Ameiliá Doherty (7)	6
Michael Allen (7)	7
Sáoirse Nic Phaidin (8)	8
Niamh Deery (7) & Lara	9
Fállon Mc Kinney (7)	10
Darragh Bradley (8) & Eibhlín	11
Connor Kelly (8)	12
Ruairí Moore (7) & Killian	13
Eamonn Harkin (7)	14

Green End Primary School, Burnage

Ivy Cawley (7)	15
Simran Chudha (6)	16
Areesha Ahmed (6)	17
Amaan Tariq (7)	18
Sharen Toni-George (6)	19

Oxford High Pre-Preparatory School, Oxford

Bisou Fiddian-Qasmiyeh (7)	20
Emilie Haith (6)	21
Chloe Liu Liu Sellers (5)	22
Emily Mitchell (5)	23
Victoria Wanner (5)	24
Jessie Kwan (7)	25

Eileen Kong (7)	26
Emilia Frise (7)	27
Victoria Mackrell (6)	28
Eliza Simpson (6)	29
Frida-Sofia von Billerbeck (7)	30
Naima Markowitz-Shulman (7)	31
Gaia Mestre (6)	32
Felicity Coupland (7)	33
Althea Chin (5)	34
Mary McFarlane (5)	35

Ravenshead CE Primary School, Ravenshead

George Bruce (7)	36
Maisy Burgess (6)	37
Elizabeth Trenchfield (7)	38
Dylan Wallace (7)	39
Zak Boulton (7)	40
Arlo Clifford (6)	41
Harvey Evans (6)	42
Amy Crofts (7)	43
Grace Taylor (7)	44
Hollie Rodham (7)	45
Lauren Pate (6)	46
Jacob Radford (7)	47
Jack Yates (6)	48
Matilda Sisson (7)	49
Jack Hopkins (7)	50
Emily Radford (7)	51
Jacob Winstanley-Jones (7)	52
Demi Hart (7)	53
Ewan O'Connell (7)	54
Zachery Metcalf (7)	55
Sofia Woodhouse (7)	56
Grace Blissett (7)	57

Thomas Cheeseman (6)	58
Henry Walker (6)	59
Molly Anderson (7)	60
Garrett Williams (6)	61
Oscar Cooper (7)	62
Dylan Booth (6)	63
Zak Moult (6)	64
Sophie Watkins (7)	65
Stanley Chambers (7)	66
Andrew Kennedy (6)	67
William Shipley (6)	68
Harry Jessop (7)	69
Oliver Scott (7)	70
Tilly Hall (6)	71
Harrison Bones (7)	72
Daniel Hall (6)	73
Eva Wiley (6)	74
Woody Charlton	75
Hamza Abougazia (7)	76
Nuala Smith (7)	77
Jasmine Faith Norbury-Lea (7)	78
Paige Koston (6)	79

Ryefield Primary School, Hillingdon

Elsie Zannini (6)	80
James Kill (7)	81
Sama Aloos (7)	82
Dev Mistry (7)	83
Ruby Stout (7)	84
Kiyana Sachdeva (7)	85
Lola Collard (6)	86
Savanna Beshi (6)	87
Viraj Singh (6)	88
Jane Ghelani-Hernando (7)	89
Emilian Ioan Cucicea (7)	90
Kaci Donnelly (7)	91
Melissa Egan (7)	92
Callum Doley (7)	93
Elsie Cole (6)	94
Yasir Jama (7)	95
Maisie Attrill (6)	96
Ryan Aliaj (7)	97

Denis Strango (6)	98
Rosie Smith (7)	99
TommyLee Mcdonagh (6)	100
Patrycja Bieniek (7)	101
Rithika Ravi (7)	102
Harry King (6)	103
Michal Chojnacki (6)	104
Ollie Peake-Stolberg (7)	105
Wissem Elguendouz (7)	106
Millie Hallett (7)	107
Ritchie Gardner (7)	108
Iqra Mukhtar (7)	109
Noah Graham (6)	110
Charlie Hughes (6)	111
Abbas Ali (7)	112

St Mary & St Joseph RC (VA) Primary School, Pocklington

Blake Woodend (7)	113
Charlotte McLaughlin (6)	114
Abbie Creaser (5)	115
Violet Houston (6)	116
Savanna Agar-Farrow (6)	117
Lewis Skelton (5)	118
Ciara Farr (6)	119
Jim Corkery (6)	120
Isabella Bellwood (6)	121
Daniel Zvinys (6)	122
Seb Hughes (5)	123
Erin Wilce (6)	124
Kian Ferry (7)	125
Tom Roelofs (5)	126

St Stephen's CE Primary School, Willington

Maisy Robson (6)	127
Embley Brunskill (6)	128
James Walker (6)	129
Ellie-May Walker (6)	130
Tammy Clough (6)	131
Riley Bell (5)	132
Thomas Hodgson (5)	133

Jacob Wise (6)	134
Charley Westmorland (5)	135

St Vincent's Catholic Primary School, Penketh

Carter Astbury (6)	136
Louie Percival (6)	137
Spencer Prockter (6)	138
Khiah Beard (7)	139
Maria Henry (7)	140
Georgia Halsall (7)	141
Noah Rigby (7)	142
Phoenix Roberts (6)	143
Hani Biviji (6)	144
Matej Kitanovski (6)	145
William Partington (6)	146
Leo Clutton (6)	147

Stonehouse Primary School, Stonehouse

Daisy Morrow (6)	148
David Gray (6)	149
Elizabeth-May Ferguson (6)	150
Halle Rodger (6)	151
Oliver Philbin (6)	152
Lily Millar (6)	153
Carly Davidson (6)	154
Finlay Steele (6)	155
Rory Kerr (6)	156
Lucy Bell (6)	157
Caylem Reynolds (6)	158
Millie Gardiner (6)	159
Eva Cameron (6)	160
Jamie Scott (6)	161
Ross Gemmell (6)	162
Poppy Summers (6)	163
Caleb McVie (6)	164
Reece Cunningham (6)	165

The Poems

Elephant

E very time I see an elephant,
L ittle elephants they spray,
E verywhere with water, they
P et you with their trunk. I
H ope you like them too.
A big elephant would be good to see,
N ext time, I hope you like
T hem too.

Fiadhna O'Neill (7)
Gaelscoil Éadain Mhóir, Brandywell

Rabbit

R abbits are so cute,
A rabbit likes to eat vegetables,
B ut they do not like ice cream!
B unny rabbit is a baby rabbit,
I have a friend who has a pet rabbit,
T he rabbits have big fluffy ears.

Mia Pirone (8)
Gaelscoil Éadain Mhóir, Brandywell

Rabbit

R abbits run fast,
A t the vet, rabbits are sick.
B ig rabbits can be white,
B ig rabbits like the sun.
I got a rabbit,
T he rabbits are so cute!

Dearbhla Devine (7)
Gaelscoil Éadain Mhóir, Brandywell

Spider

S ome spiders are big,
P et spiders are cute.
I got a spider as a pet,
D o you like spiders?
E very spider is cute,
R eally, really cute!

Cayden Williams (7)
Gaelscoil Éadain Mhóir, Brandywell

Dog

D o you like dogs? Well, I love them!
O h well, I will tell you all about them, they are fluffy.
G o on and get one. They are cute, white, friendly, small and playful.

Caislín Clarke (8)
Gaelscoil Éadain Mhóir, Brandywell

Monkey

M oves a lot,
O nly likes bananas,
N o monkeys are pandas.
K ind of bad,
E asy to feed,
Y ou like monkeys too.

Ameiliá Doherty (7)
Gaelscoil Éadain Mhóir, Brandywell

Wolf

W olves are cute and fun,
O ld men don't like wolves.
L eave them alone so,
F olk can stay alive!

Michael Allen (7)
Gaelscoil Éadain Mhóir, Brandywell

Dog

D o you like small brown dogs?
O h my goodness, I can have a dog.
G etting a dog is fun.

Sáoirse Nic Phaidin (8)
Gaelscoil Éadain Mhóir, Brandywell

Cat

C an I have a cat?
A cat is the cutest animal.
T hat boy has lots of cats.

Niamh Deery (7) & Lara
Gaelscoil Éadain Mhóir, Brandywell

Dog

D o you like small brown dogs?
O ld dogs are nice,
G etting a dog is fun.

Fállon Mc Kinney (7)
Gaelscoil Éadain Mhóir, Brandywell

Dog

D o you have a dog?
O h my goodness, I can have a dog,
G od made you.

Darragh Bradley (8) & Eibhlín
Gaelscoil Éadain Mhóir, Brandywell

Cat

C an I get a cat?
A cat is the cutest,
T he old man has five cats.

Connor Kelly (8)
Gaelscoil Éadain Mhóir, Brandywell

Dog

D ogs are fun,
O ld man's best friend,
G reatest dog ever.

Ruairí Moore (7) & Killian
Gaelscoil Éadain Mhóir, Brandywell

Cat

C ats are orange,
A nd afraid of dogs,
T reats please, oh yes!

Eamonn Harkin (7)
Gaelscoil Éadain Mhóir, Brandywell

Unicorn

U nder the bright blue sky, where the birds fly high,
N earby where the trees sway in the summer breeze,
I ncredible unicorns there like to pleasure and please.
C olourful flowers blossoming everywhere,
O n clouds, the unicorns admire their beautiful hair.
R are sparkly horn shining like a star,
N ibbling on rainbow dust while granting every child's wish.

Ivy Cawley (7)
Green End Primary School, Burnage

Unicorn

U nicorns are very different,
N ice and beautiful,
I love unicorns so much, they're my favourite animal.
C arry happiness and make me happy,
O h, I wish I could see one for real.
R ainbow features they have white, red, green, pink, blue, white and
N obody thinks they are real.

Simran Chudha (6)
Green End Primary School, Burnage

A Cheeky Monkey

M onkeys are cheeky and clever,
O ften monkeys live in forests or jungles,
N othing scares a monkey.
K now that a monkey is clever,
E levated above the ground is where they live,
Y ou can communicate with a monkey and they will understand.

Areesha Ahmed (6)
Green End Primary School, Burnage

The Fierce Tiger

T riple in energy and
I nstant in attack.
G ood at hunting,
E specially in hungry times,
R oyal in nature.

Amaan Tariq (7)
Green End Primary School, Burnage

Kitten

K etchup
I s
T errifically
T idy
E very day and
N ow.

Sharen Toni-George (6)
Green End Primary School, Burnage

Colossal Squid

C olossal creature with luminous limbs,
O range tentacles to trap its prey.
L ooking here, looking there,
O bserving, looking everywhere.
S wirling and swooping through the sea,
S lowly emerging from the deep.
A s it swims through the waves, so bitingly cold,
L ike a shimmering lightning bolt.

S oaring slyly towards the sun,
Q uivering queen of the coral reef.
U nderneath the ocean, it loops and twirls.
I n its beauty it is alone,
D esigned for the depths, this is its home.

Bisou Fiddian-Qasmiyeh (7)
Oxford High Pre-Preparatory School, Oxford

Giant Pandas!

G iant pandas!
I love giant pandas,
A nd they love to play.
N ibbling bamboo all day,
T hey wear black and white suits.

P ink baby pandas are ever so cute,
A nd they come from China,
N apping all day makes everything seem finer.
D id you know that pandas do lots and lots of poos?
A nyone can see them in the zoo.

Emilie Haith (6)
Oxford High Pre-Preparatory School, Oxford

A Magical Cat

A cat is hungry.

M useum is open,
A cat show is on,
G ood food is there,
I t looks very yummy,
C at comes in,
A nd eats all of the food,
L ater the cat magics a park.

C at is very happy,
A magical cat is having fun,
T omorrow the magical cat will be back again.

Chloe Liu Liu Sellers (5)
Oxford High Pre-Preparatory School, Oxford

Butterfly

B eautiful butterfly,
U nder the swooshing colours the butterfly dances,
T he butterfly makes pretty patterns.
T wirling bluebells ring,
E veryone loves the butterfly's dances.
R oses are bobbing along,
F lowers are spinning.
L ovely sights making us all happy,
Y ellow sparkles in the air.

Emily Mitchell (5)
Oxford High Pre-Preparatory School, Oxford

Flying Unicorns

U nicorns are sparkly,
N ight stars are twinkling.
I n the dark forest, hearts are lying on the ground,
C an pink unicorns dance on rainbows, blinking?
O ur unicorns are in our ideas,
R ainbow-coloured manes up high.
N ever seen them with pretty wings,
S hooting stars shooting through the sky.

Victoria Wanner (5)
Oxford High Pre-Preparatory School, Oxford

Peacock Poem

P eaceful birds spreading their gorgeous wings,
E legantly walking up and down.
A cting like a king showing off,
C hirping like a famous singer.
O pening their fascinating feathers like a fan,
C aring for their peachicks,
K ing of all the beautiful birds.

Jessie Kwan (7)
Oxford High Pre-Preparatory School, Oxford

Unicorn Umpire

U nique mane and tail,
N ever-ending grail.
I nteresting colour-changing eyes,
C an coast along to lovely rhymes.
O lder ones are powerful,
R ummaging through the small seagulls.
N ot allowed to push aside,
S ockets always must provide!

Eileen Kong (7)
Oxford High Pre-Preparatory School, Oxford

The Alicorn's Adventure

A beautiful alicorn soaring across the skies
L ooks, sees and can't believe her eyes
I nky blue sea, deep and wide
C rashing, curly waves splashing with the tide
O h what a beautiful view I see
R ough waves all around me
N o to being normal.

Emilia Frise (7)
Oxford High Pre-Preparatory School, Oxford

Rabbit, Rabbit

R abbit, rabbit,
A re you white or brown?
B rown like the darkest night,
B aby rabbit, where are your mummy and daddy?
I don't know, maybe they are bouncing in the meadows.
T hank you baby rabbit, bye-bye!

Victoria Mackrell (6)
Oxford High Pre-Preparatory School, Oxford

Izzy The Giraffe

G randma has a giraffe at home,
I zzy is her name.
R ather cheeky,
A lso tall,
F eet that go stomp, stomp.
F luffy-tailed Izzy once did an
E rrand for Grandma. Oh no! Her tail got stuck in the door!

Eliza Simpson (6)
Oxford High Pre-Preparatory School, Oxford

The Little Tiger Poem

T errifying tigers that roar non-stop,
I tty-bitty tigers that always flop.
G rr because they are very mad,
E ven when they are very glad.
R oar say the tigers, that makes my heart drop.

Frida-Sofia von Billerbeck (7)
Oxford High Pre-Preparatory School, Oxford

King Of Africa

L urking in the hot haze,
I n the glistening blaze, he lays.
O ver everyone he watches, for King he is named,
N o one dares to touch his precious mane.

Naima Markowitz-Shulman (7)
Oxford High Pre-Preparatory School, Oxford

Wolf

W oods are full of wolves,
O ut they come at night.
L ots of wolves in the world,
F illing the quiet with their howling.

Gaia Mestre (6)
Oxford High Pre-Preparatory School, Oxford

Dolphin

D iving in
O ceans blue.
L eaping
P layfully,
H igh
I nto the
N ight.

Felicity Coupland (7)
Oxford High Pre-Preparatory School, Oxford

Cats

C ats meow, cats purr, cats sleep.
A lot of fish and mice they eat,
T hey have paws instead of feet.

Althea Chin (5)
Oxford High Pre-Preparatory School, Oxford

Listen To The Lion

L oud, noisy lion,
I n the jungle.
O n the grass,
N ow she is roaring!

Mary McFarlane (5)
Oxford High Pre-Preparatory School, Oxford

My Cute Guinea Pig

G uinea pigs like carrots and lettuce
U nlike if they ate meat
I n their hutch, they are cute
N ever biting anyone because they are so lovely
E ven though they may get cross
A nd nibble through the bars

P igs like to sniff and snort
I have pigs but they are cute
G uinea pigs are the best!

George Bruce (7)
Ravenshead CE Primary School, Ravenshead

Hippo

B rilliant, big in the swamp,
A mazing, enthusiastic, eating his dinner here comes a chomp in a one, two, three...
B rave and strong, wanting to be the winner, just wait here because I need to go and get some beer,
Y ay, the fun is beginning, ho-oh, so I better go, see ya.

H appy, hot hippo scaring the animals,
I ncredible, big, helpful - wouldn't you agree?
P retty and perfect in the pool with his friends,
P laying in the mud,
O ver the mountains into the mud.

Maisy Burgess (6)
Ravenshead CE Primary School, Ravenshead

My Beautiful Butterfly

B utterflies are extremely beautiful and pretty
U tterly beautiful butterflies flap their wings
T urning elegantly on the flower
T iny butterfly flies through the sky
E xtremely stunning with magnificent wings
R eady to land on a colourful flower
F lying happily to get home
L ife is amazing as a beautiful butterfly
Y ou would love to live the life of a butterfly.

Elizabeth Trenchfield (7)
Ravenshead CE Primary School, Ravenshead

My Rattling Rattlesnake

R attlesnakes go *hiss! Hiss! Hiss!*
A nd when they strike they miss!
T hey rattle a warning,
T hey bite if you don't listen.
L ying there they might play dead,
E ven though they have a strong head.
S o don't go near rattlesnakes,
N ever touch,
A nd you might hear the grown-ups say,
K eep doing what they say,
E very day!

Dylan Wallace (7)
Ravenshead CE Primary School, Ravenshead

Blue Whale

B ig blue whale swimming gracefully,
L oud whale gliding nicely and happily.
U nique, special and very kind,
E ver so lovely having all his friends in mind.

W hile the whale loves to eat,
H e taps his fins to the wonderful beat.
A wesome, tremendous and rather large too,
L ots of food means a big poo!
E ven he swims through to the end.

Zak Boulton (7)
Ravenshead CE Primary School, Ravenshead

My Rapid Crocodile

C reeping crocs are bad today when they are,
R apid and waiting for their prey.
O ften they bite and they like being in the sun,
C rocs are usually lonely!
O ld crocodiles are a bit weak,
D own they go to the swamp where they like it.
I dle, scaly crocodiles you can see,
L ying down on the beach they can be seen,
E ating their prey!

Arlo Clifford (6)
Ravenshead CE Primary School, Ravenshead

Koala Bear

K ind, caring, fluffy and cute,
O h look at them eating their fruit.
A mazing mammals, as they are so clever,
L ook at them sleeping in their layers of leather.
A s you can't resist them,

B ecause they're so fluffy.
E ven though they eat eucalyptus leaves,
A nd they pray for peace,
R emarkable and amazing.

Harvey Evans (6)
Ravenshead CE Primary School, Ravenshead

My Fierce Crocodile

C reeping quietly in the hedge,
R eally close to the edge,
O f the stinky, smelly swamp,
C roc eyes his prey and his tail goes whomp.
O nly he knows what he's done,
D ripping off to his cave he said,
"I 'll have a fun day tomorrow!"
L eaping loudly, searching for prey,
E ating it up all day.

Amy Crofts (7)
Ravenshead CE Primary School, Ravenshead

My Cute Koala Bear

K ing koala gently snuggles,
O h being a koala, it is lovely,
A koala is special, cuddly and cute.
L ovely and fun to boot,
A cuddly koala is lazy all day.

B rave koalas climb the tree to stay safe,
E ek! They are amazing too,
A nd don't have to wear any shoes,
R eally, they are cute!

Grace Taylor (7)
Ravenshead CE Primary School, Ravenshead

Koala Bear

K ind, fluffy, cute, adorable,
O h, watch them eating their dinner and fruit.
A mazing animals,
L eaping koalas like to travel,
A s you know, they are cute as can be.

B ecause they are so happy,
E legant and sleepy.
A lways sleepy sitting in a tree,
R eady to find its tea.

Hollie Rodham (7)
Ravenshead CE Primary School, Ravenshead

Barn Owls

B arn owls at night eat their prey,
A nd barn owls sleep in the day.
R ain hurts barn owl's skin very badly,
N ow we hear the barn owls sing.

O ne hoot, two hoots, hear him swoop,
W hen you hear him click and hoop.
L ook he flies with a slam,
S ee his friends on the way.

Lauren Pate (6)
Ravenshead CE Primary School, Ravenshead

My Exuberant Elephant

E lephants stomp with big feet,
L oving to eat juicy meat,
E lephants have a long grey trunk,
P hew, it means they can't get sunk.
H e goes for a walk,
A nd has some fun,
N ever burning in the sun.
T heir trunks are very good,
S tare at an elephant!

Jacob Radford (7)
Ravenshead CE Primary School, Ravenshead

Tiger

T igers have terribly bad and sharp claws,
I n fact, they are nowhere near as terrible as their jaws.
G rasslands that is their home, they meet all their friends,
E ven on a weekend they run around the bends,
"R oar!" said the tiger. "I'm very fair and will defend."

Jack Yates (6)
Ravenshead CE Primary School, Ravenshead

My Joyful Elephant

E legantly they walk down the path,
L anding their big feet forward.
E ven stomping through the leaves,
P ouncing is a no, no, no!
H andy is their middle name,
A nd the thing is big.
N ow in the future, it may not be big,
T he thing loves its family.

Matilda Sisson (7)
Ravenshead CE Primary School, Ravenshead

Gorilla

G reat gorilla swings in the tree
O bviously he is hungry and wants his tea
R aging and cross as he has no food
I nstead, he wears his sunglasses like a dude
L ook over there, off he goes
L oving the jungle he lives in
A mazing gorilla, he never has any woes.

Jack Hopkins (7)
Ravenshead CE Primary School, Ravenshead

Giraffe

G igantic, long giraffe has lots of spots,
I n the jungle it likes to trot.
R esting in his snuggly bed,
A dorable giraffe rests his long head.
F antastic, all animals around him want some hay,
F rosty snow in the winter bay,
E ating trees and munching away.

Emily Radford (7)
Ravenshead CE Primary School, Ravenshead

My Lovely Butterfly

B eautiful and light,
U nique in flight,
T ypical wings tingle,
T hey are double not single.
E njoyment and excitement, they
R ace rapidly but don't
F all.
L onely they glide in the air,
Y esterday I saw one on a chair!

Jacob Winstanley-Jones (7)
Ravenshead CE Primary School, Ravenshead

My Gentle Giraffe

G iraffes are tall and they have big hooves,
I 'd rather stretch up and eat my tea.
R eally think their necks are too tall,
A nd their orange colour is not good at all.
F earless and brave,
F orever they are,
E ven at night in the dark.

Demi Hart (7)
Ravenshead CE Primary School, Ravenshead

Whales

W ild and free and swimming in the sea,
H appily as always and as can be.
A wesome, elegant, his favourite drink is tea,
L aughing loudly with his friends with glee.
E very day he slowly finds his food,
S o that he never gets in a terrible mood!

Ewan O'Connell (7)
Ravenshead CE Primary School, Ravenshead

My Awkward Octopus

O ctopuses are ugly and angry,
C oiling arms, very tangly.
T hrough the rocks they spy,
O n fish and snails who hide.
P ulling prey into a beaky grin,
U nless they go too fast for him.
S wimming to shore, he catches a fish or more!

Zachery Metcalf (7)
Ravenshead CE Primary School, Ravenshead

Panda

P retty panda wakes up and wants some lunch
A nd he's eating bamboo and making a crunch
N ice panda sits down and is nice and still
D ark now, pandas are naughty and behaviour goes downhill
A nd finally, he's tucked in bed, safe and sound.

Sofia Woodhouse (7)
Ravenshead CE Primary School, Ravenshead

Elephant

E llie the elephant likes to play,
L ong through the day.
E ats grass along the path,
P eacefully having a bath.
H uge stompy feet,
A lways likes to eat meat.
N ice friendly animals,
T hat really like to travel.

Grace Blissett (7)
Ravenshead CE Primary School, Ravenshead

Tiger

T iger likes it in a tree,
I know Tom is fast and curious, just like me.
G et to know him and he may be mad and bad.
"E ek!" said the tiger. "You need to stop being mad,
R ight you little monkey, stop being sad."

Thomas Cheeseman (6)
Ravenshead CE Primary School, Ravenshead

My Terrifying Tiger

T errifying, scary, don't you see? He's
I n the plants, running free.
G rowling loudly, catching prey, he
E ats it hungrily every day. He's
R oaring loud, you cannot miss,
S cary tiger, you wouldn't kiss!

Henry Walker (6)
Ravenshead CE Primary School, Ravenshead

Monkey

M agnificent and clever when eating leaves,
O bservant monkey swings off trees.
N atural monkeys like to scoff,
K ind when not a show-off.
E xcited, kind, when it wants to be,
Y awning when tired, swinging off trees.

Molly Anderson (7)
Ravenshead CE Primary School, Ravenshead

Dinos

D inos find their prey a lot of time in the wild
I t is not good if they can't get food
N ever should you come close because they'll crunch your feet
O ften they'll roar and you'll be scared away
S o I go away!

Garrett Williams (6)
Ravenshead CE Primary School, Ravenshead

Tiger

T houghtless tiger sitting in a tree,
I t wants to go and can't wait to see.
G reat dinner he searches for high and low,
E ven though he is sometimes a little too slow,
R emember the tiger will never ever be full of woe.

Oscar Cooper (7)
Ravenshead CE Primary School, Ravenshead

My Excitable Monkey

M onkeys always swing around,
O n the branches and on the ground.
N oisy, scampering on the slippery floor,
K icking away from the door.
E ager to eat juicy fruit,
Y et never chews on smelly boots.

Dylan Booth (6)
Ravenshead CE Primary School, Ravenshead

My Amazing Shark

S harks swim so really fast,
H olidays is the best place to see them.
A t last, their eyes watch them,
R emember to swim quietly away,
K eep your cool when you see a grey fin, careful or they will bite!

Zak Moult (6)
Ravenshead CE Primary School, Ravenshead

Tiger

T onight I am lucky, the prey is standing there,
I n the wild it's incredibly fair.
G reat awesome tiger,
E xcitedly he goes to catch his prey for tea,
R oaring tiger can sometimes be a monster.

Sophie Watkins (7)
Ravenshead CE Primary School, Ravenshead

Bunny

B unny rabbits are extremely cute,
U nique and wonderful, he wears boots.
N ever dirty and always a joy,
N aughty isn't his thing even though he's a boy,
Y ou will always be happy with you.

Stanley Chambers (7)
Ravenshead CE Primary School, Ravenshead

My Shocking Cheetah

C heetahs run like light,
H eaps of people hide,
E merge from hiding,
E ek! With fear.
T o you, it runs,
A t great speed,
H e kills prey,
S caring you of course!

Andrew Kennedy (6)
Ravenshead CE Primary School, Ravenshead

Monkey

M ischievous, fluffy, cute,
O n the trees they eat crunchy leaves.
N aughty, cheeky, they are,
K ind and wild, they cheat.
E very monkey likes to play,
Y ellow bananas left on a tray.

William Shipley (6)
Ravenshead CE Primary School, Ravenshead

My Mucky Hippo

H ippos are large and grey,
I nside the mud they like to
P lay, proud, mucky, wrinkly and wise,
P lease bear in mind they might give you a surprise,
O nly professionals should look after them.

Harry Jessop (7)
Ravenshead CE Primary School, Ravenshead

Zebra

Z ak the zebra zigzags across the plains
E legantly swishing his long mane
B eautiful, elegant and good to look at
R emember, don't look at his earwax
A lso, beware, never pays his tax.

Oliver Scott (7)
Ravenshead CE Primary School, Ravenshead

Zebra

Z ebras might seem cute but they're quiet,
E nergetic and have a good diet.
B anging zebras are hungry for their food,
R aising up to the moon,
A mazing, outstanding zebras.

Tilly Hall (6)
Ravenshead CE Primary School, Ravenshead

My Little Lizard

L izards are fun in the sun,
I n the trees it spies
Z ebra!
A lot it sees,
R ed roses in the trees,
D own on the ground it's not fast.

Harrison Bones (7)
Ravenshead CE Primary School, Ravenshead

My Ferocious Sabretooth

T iger once had sabretooth,
I n a time, long ago.
G rowling loud around,
E ach one goes,
R acing to get some fish,
S uch a lovely dish!

Daniel Hall (6)
Ravenshead CE Primary School, Ravenshead

My Grand Tiger

T igers are very fierce,
I llness will never get them,
G rand animals have big sharp teeth.
E vil enemies beware, the tiger will get
R abbits!

Eva Wiley (6)
Ravenshead CE Primary School, Ravenshead

Sloth

S low with sharp claws
L oving with cute paws
O ften sleeping in the trees
T he sloth is as happy as can be
H ow it is to be like me!

Woody Charlton
Ravenshead CE Primary School, Ravenshead

My Little Fish

F rightened fish flicked through the pool,
I know that fish.
S hiny lovely shapes amaze,
H ow beautiful its scales, in so many ways.

Hamza Abougazia (7)
Ravenshead CE Primary School, Ravenshead

Lion

L ong, mean and a bit tall,
I llness, the lion falls.
O ld, yellow and brave,
N one would find them if they were hiding in a cave.

Nuala Smith (7)
Ravenshead CE Primary School, Ravenshead

My Friendly Owl

O wls are cool,
W hen they fly after prey.
L oudly they cry,
S wooping, hooting, they fly!

Jasmine Faith Norbury-Lea (7)
Ravenshead CE Primary School, Ravenshead

My Cute T-Rex

T -rex is big and strong
R eally scary!
E xcept if you are bigger
X ylophones are smaller!

Paige Koston (6)
Ravenshead CE Primary School, Ravenshead

Aqua Dragons

A quatic swimmers under the blue sea,
Q uick swimmers under the deep, dark sea,
U nder the sea, there are some Aqua Dragons,
A mazing, peaceful swimmers.

D ragons are amazing acrobats,
R eally amazing acrobats under the sea,
A crobats under the beautiful sea,
G razing under the sea,
O ften swimming in the dark sea,
N ever leaving the sea.

Elsie Zannini (6)
Ryefield Primary School, Hillingdon

Under The Ocean

A mazing colourful dragon in the sea,
Q uietly around the dark blue sea.
U seful and fast in the dark deep ocean,
A rchaic in the wide ocean.

D esolate in the colourful ocean,
R esilient under the blue ocean,
A mazing under the archaic rusty sea.
G reat colourful swimmers,
O penly gliding in the ocean,
N ow a dragon is coming to town.

James Kill (7)
Ryefield Primary School, Hillingdon

The Amazing Pets

A stonishing creature of all,
Q ueue up for the amazing fish,
U pside down, loopy-loop and off they go,
A lovely present for the class.

D own and up off the clean tank,
R ight and left, up and down,
A group of fish that are all friends,
G o swimming and never give up,
O n the go, looking for food,
N ever give up for anything.

Sama Aloos (7)
Ryefield Primary School, Hillingdon

Colourful Creatures

A qua Dragons are energetic, positive swimmers,
Q uietly fast, quick swimmers,
U nderwater swimmers only,
A lways moving for scrummy food.

D angerous, hungry swimmers,
R esourceful, energetic swimmers,
A wesome swimmers in the water,
G enerous creatures in the deep sea,
O n the watch for yummy food,
N on-violent creature.

Dev Mistry (7)
Ryefield Primary School, Hillingdon

Aqua Dragons

A mazing underwater swimmers,
Q uietly swimming through,
U nder the sea, Aqua Dragons are found,
A ll over the world in the ocean.

D ragons can swim, their names are Aqua Dragons,
R ooting for food all over the sea,
A quatic swimmers in the ocean,
G lorious animals are they,
O h, under the beautiful sea,
N ot a peep!

Ruby Stout (7)
Ryefield Primary School, Hillingdon

Water Monkeys

A mazing dragons swimming underwater,
Q uick swimming in the big ocean,
U nderwater, they're swimming,
A nimals that live underwater.

D eep diving and wet,
R eal swimmers, fast for fish,
A nimals underwater,
G reat splashing in the ocean,
O n the watch for food,
N ever get out.

Kiyana Sachdeva (7)
Ryefield Primary School, Hillingdon

Undersea World

A dragon is under the sea,
Q uietly splashing and growing,
U nder the sea, swimming quickly,
A little bit fast and cold.

D ragon is feeling lonely,
R unning quickly and swimming,
A dragon is lonely,
G reat swimmers under the sea,
O n the seaweed,
N ot lonely but with friends.

Lola Collard (6)
Ryefield Primary School, Hillingdon

Under The Sea

A round the wide, blue oceans,
Q uietly swimming.
U nder the wonderful sea,
A mazing swimmers under the blue sea.

D elicate, amazing animals,
R esourceful little creatures.
A dorable magical creatures,
G reat lovely animals.
O n the watch for bad enemies,
N o eating big animals.

Savanna Beshi (6)
Ryefield Primary School, Hillingdon

Aqua Dragons

A mazing swimming moves that are so fast,
Q uietly swimming,
U seful creatures,
A mbitious creatures,

D o not move the tank,
R eally small creatures getting bigger every day,
A mazing creatures to see,
G orgeous these are, big,
O n the lookout for tasty food,
N ever scare them!

Viraj Singh (6)
Ryefield Primary School, Hillingdon

Aqua Dragons

A mazing to see them swim,
Q uiet, fantastic swimmers,
U p and down and round about,
A re they really big?

D o they breathe underwater?
R unning across the water,
A cross the water swimming,
G oing around and around,
O n the lookout for delicacies,
N ever rude to their father.

Jane Ghelani-Hernando (7)
Ryefield Primary School, Hillingdon

Aqua Dragons

A mazing, outstanding swimmers,
Q uick swimmers in the ocean,
U nder the dark blue sea,
A mazing dragon.

D ragon of water,
R elaxed Aqua Dragons,
A crobatic, quick swimmers,
G reat swimmers,
O ctopus hunter,
N ever giving up,
S wimming like a megalodon.

Emilian Ioan Cucicea (7)
Ryefield Primary School, Hillingdon

Rainbow Shine

A see-through animal in water,
Q ueen of the water,
U p and in the water,
A mazing animals in the water,

D eep in the water and floats,
R unning and bashing for food,
A nimals that are fast,
G ood at swimming
O n the water for food,
N earby, swimming.

Kaci Donnelly (7)
Ryefield Primary School, Hillingdon

Wonderful Skinny Sea Creatures

A fantastic swimmer,
Q ueen of the sea creatures,
U nderwater animal,
A mazing swimming animal,

D uring the day they never sleep,
R ule of the queen sea animal,
A n underwater swimmer,
G o on the roll,
O n the go,
N o harm to our sea animals.

Melissa Egan (7)
Ryefield Primary School, Hillingdon

The Swimmers

A mazing racing as fast as lightning,
Q uizzical creatures,
U nderwater swimmers,
A stonishing eaters,

D isaster to not do work,
R acing into each other,
A nimals are funny,
G oing out of control,
O n the watch for others,
N o, wait for you!

Callum Doley (7)
Ryefield Primary School, Hillingdon

The Aqua Dragons

A water animal,
Q uietly sneak up,
U nderwater swimmer,
A mazing swimmer.

D uring the day they swim lots,
R unning like lightning,
A dventures that they can't do,
G oing in circles,
O n the watch for people,
N ever get out of the tank.

Elsie Cole (6)
Ryefield Primary School, Hillingdon

Fast Aqua Dragons

A mazing swimmers through the sea,
Q uick swimmers, better than humans.
U nder the sea,
A wesome swimmers.

D ragon swims fast,
R ushing swimmer,
A qua Dragons are great swimmers.
G reat swimmer,
O n the watch for a meal,
N ice Aqua Dragon.

Yasir Jama (7)
Ryefield Primary School, Hillingdon

The Aqua Dragons

A mazing at flips,
Q uite funny and lazy,
U nderwater home,
A weird creature in the world.

D oing things in the water,
R eady to rumble,
A mbitious at finding food,
G reedy and funny,
O n the watch for seafood,
N ever leave their tank.

Maisie Attrill (6)
Ryefield Primary School, Hillingdon

My First Acrostic: Animal Adventures - Future Voices

Aqua Dragons

A mazing swimmers,
Q uiet dragons in the sea,
U nder the ocean,
A mbitious divers.

D estroyers of fish,
R eally small and big,
A dorable dragons,
G oing to hatch in the ocean,
O n the watch for fish,
N ever get out of water.

Ryan Aliaj (7)
Ryefield Primary School, Hillingdon

Silly Monkey

A mazing animal in the sea,
Q uizzical sea animal,
U nderwater sea creature,
A tiny animal in the sea.

D iving for food,
R obust sea creature,
A mazing creature,
G oing for food,
O n the watch for food,
N ormal sea animal.

Denis Strango (6)
Ryefield Primary School, Hillingdon

Amazing Swimmers!

A mazing, resilient sea creatures,
Q uality swimmers,
U nder the sea queen,
A mazing, calm sea creatures.

D ancing swimmers,
R obust breathers,
A mbitious pets,
G ood swimmers,
O n the watch for food,
N ice at swimming.

Rosie Smith (7)
Ryefield Primary School, Hillingdon

Aqua Dragons

A water-made swimmer,
Q uick and super fast,
U nderwater catching food,
A qua Dragons are funny!

D oing funny things,
R unning fast,
A re very hungry,
G oing to find friends,
O n the water, swimming,
N ever ever fight.

TommyLee Mcdonagh (6)
Ryefield Primary School, Hillingdon

My First Acrostic: Animal Adventures - Future Voices

Amazing Aqua Dragons

A mazing swimmer,
Q uiet runner,
U nderwater breather,
A bumper into each other,

D iving creatures,
R ight in the brain,
A salty water liver,
G oing to marry soon,
O n the need for things,
N ever move the tank.

Patrycja Bieniek (7)
Ryefield Primary School, Hillingdon

Aqua Dragon: Team Dragon

A n underwater animal,
Q uiet for me,
U ltra-rare,
A mazing water animal.

D uring the day they sleep,
R eally in love,
A mbitious finders,
G one to the surface to eat,
O n the hunt for food,
N eed to find love.

Rithika Ravi (7)
Ryefield Primary School, Hillingdon

The Aqua Dragon

A mazing in the fantastic water,
Q ueen in the water,
U nderwater they swim quick,
A lovely dragon,

D ancing in the water,
R ocking in the water,
A fantastic
G rumbly creature,
O n top of it a
N ice animal.

Harry King (6)
Ryefield Primary School, Hillingdon

Fast, Go

A lways small,
Q ueen of the water,
U nderwater breathing,
A s small as an ant,

D ive quickly,
R acing as fast as a tiger,
A mazing, see-through creature,
G reat swimmer,
O n each other,
N aughty creatures.

Michal Chojnacki (6)
Ryefield Primary School, Hillingdon

Sea Creatures

A mazing creatures,
Q uizzical creatures,
U nder the sea queen,
A mbitious creatures,

D angerous breathing,
R obust swimmers,
A ngry as can be,
G ood swimmers,
O n the hunt for food,
N ow it's bedtime.

Ollie Peake-Stolberg (7)
Ryefield Primary School, Hillingdon

Quickly Ambitious Animals

A mazing underwater swimmers,
Q ueen of the tank,
U ltra-light animals,
A dorable creatures,

D iving underwater,
R are creatures,
A mbitious creatures,
G lorious animals,
O ff they go,
N ever give up.

Wissem Elguendouz (7)
Ryefield Primary School, Hillingdon

Aqua Dragon

A beautiful swimmer,
Q uick swimmer,
U nder the beautiful ocean,
A qua Dragons are so fast.

D ark blue waves,
R acing after animals,
A quiet swimmer.
G ood swimmers,
O cean waving,
N ight swimmers.

Millie Hallett (7)
Ryefield Primary School, Hillingdon

Aqua Dragon

A mazing camouflage,
Q uick swimmers.
U nder the water,
A mazing dragons.

D esolate dragon,
R oaring above the waves.
A mazing colours,
G row amazingly.
O n the watch for fish,
N o enemies.

Ritchie Gardner (7)
Ryefield Primary School, Hillingdon

Little Fish, Little Fish

A little fish,
Q ueen of the water,
U nderwater swimmers,
A cute animal,

D on't go down,
R un fast,
A cute pet,
G et thin,
O n the watch for food,
N ever hungry.

Iqra Mukhtar (7)
Ryefield Primary School, Hillingdon

Amazing Aqua Dragon

A mazing and special,
Q ueen of the water,
U sed to swimming,
A cool flip.

D ancing,
R un fast,
A boss,
G reat creature,
O n the hunt for food,
N o leaving the tank.

Noah Graham (6)
Ryefield Primary School, Hillingdon

My Cat

C harlie's cat hides,
A ctually a chatty cat,
T ail swings backwards and forwards.

Charlie Hughes (6)
Ryefield Primary School, Hillingdon

The Dog

D ig for bones,
O utside in the sunny park,
G entle and playful.

Abbas Ali (7)
Ryefield Primary School, Hillingdon

The Enormous Crocodile

C *runch munch*, eating little children.
R ough, tough and fierce.
O ne child is not enough.
C lever tricks and secret plans.
O ff he goes to the coconut trees.
D isguised as a coconut tree with a sly smile.
I t pretends to be a see-saw.
L ying in wait for a child.
E normous crocodile's sharp white teeth like a sword.

Blake Woodend (7)
St Mary & St Joseph RC (VA) Primary School, Pocklington

Flying Albatross

A lways gracefully gliding, where are you going?
L ongest wingspan of all birds.
B ig feet!
A mazing at flying.
T iny, fluffy, fuzzy babies.
R eally bad at landing.
O range beaks!
S oft, white feathers.
S uper nest-builders.

Charlotte McLaughlin (6)
St Mary & St Joseph RC (VA) Primary School, Pocklington

Dolphins

D olphins have dorsal fins on their backs.
O ften playful.
L ogging is when dolphins sleep.
P od is the name for a group of dolphins.
H ave a friendly nature,
I ntelligent mammals.
N ever chew, they swallow fish whole.

Abbie Creaser (5)
St Mary & St Joseph RC (VA) Primary School, Pocklington

Dolphin In The Sea

D ive, why do they dive? How do they dive?
O cean, why do they live in the ocean?
L ovely.
P layful, why are they playful?
H appy, aren't they happy?
I ntelligent.
N ice. Why are they nice? Aren't they nice?

Violet Houston (6)
St Mary & St Joseph RC (VA) Primary School, Pocklington

The Rainbow Cat

K ittens are cute and cuddly.
I ntelligent means very clever.
T ails that swish really nicely and slowly.
T ired after playing with my dog at home.
E xplores the home upstairs and downstairs.
N ice to everybody every day.

Savanna Agar-Farrow (6)
St Mary & St Joseph RC (VA) Primary School, Pocklington

Cat And Dog Catch The Frog

D aring.
O bedient.
G uard dog.

C ute.
A dorable.
T abby.

F rog, where are you going?
R *ibbit. Ribbit.*
O ver there is the pond.
G reen and slimy.

Lewis Skelton (5)
St Mary & St Joseph RC (VA) Primary School, Pocklington

Elephant Talk

E legant when they walk.
L ong trunk to drink with.
E at lots of food.
P uts water over his back.
H e has a hairy back.
A ble to pull leaves off trees.
N eeds water to live.
T usks to fight.

Ciara Farr (6)
St Mary & St Joseph RC (VA) Primary School, Pocklington

The Humongous Dinosaur

D angerous.
I n the past but
N ow they are extinct
O r
S o we think.
A thing that's fierce.
U nder the ground
R emains a fossil or not.

Jim Corkery (6)
St Mary & St Joseph RC (VA) Primary School, Pocklington

Clingy Koala

K oalas are fluffy and cute.
O nly eating bamboo.
A lways fluffy.
L ove each other.
A lways clingy.

Why are koalas clingy?
Why do koalas hang off trees?

Isabella Bellwood (6)
St Mary & St Joseph RC (VA) Primary School, Pocklington

Zoo

Z oo is a big place where you can see
E ach individual's stripes are unique
B ody length is 2.2-2.5m
R iding wouldn't be practical.
A ll for one and one for all!

Daniel Zvinys (6)
St Mary & St Joseph RC (VA) Primary School, Pocklington

All About Tigers

T hey have stripy coats,
I ndia is one of its homes,
G rown-up tigers can jump ten metres,
E ating is one of their favourite things,
R oaring makes them scary.

Seb Hughes (5)
St Mary & St Joseph RC (VA) Primary School, Pocklington

The Scary Bear

B ear is beastly, don't be scared.
E verything goes quiet.
A ll around the woods.
R oars ring out loud.

Why is the bear roaring?

Erin Wilce (6)
St Mary & St Joseph RC (VA) Primary School, Pocklington

Bouncy Rabbit

R unning rabbit.
A nimal.
B ouncy, why do they bounce?
B een eating carrots.
I nteresting.
T ired of bouncing.

Kian Ferry (7)
St Mary & St Joseph RC (VA) Primary School, Pocklington

Camel

C arry heavy weights.
A sian camels have two humps.
M ammal.
E ats plants.
L ong legs.

Tom Roelofs (5)
St Mary & St Joseph RC (VA) Primary School, Pocklington

Unicorn

U nbelievable unicorn
N ice unicorn
I n the sky
C ute unicorn
O ut into the sky
R ainbow hair
N oisily purring.

Maisy Robson (6)
St Stephen's CE Primary School, Willington

Unicorn

U nbelievable, fluffy,
N ice hair,
I ncredible magic.
C ute eyes,
O range tail.
R uns fast,
N eat horn.

Embley Brunskill (6)
St Stephen's CE Primary School, Willington

Rabbit

R eally fluffy,
A rabbit is beautiful.
B ig rabbit,
B eautiful bouncy rabbit.
I t is very nice,
T iny friend.

James Walker (6)
St Stephen's CE Primary School, Willington

Rabbit

R un fast,
A mazing jumper,
B eautiful rabbit.
B ig ears,
I s soft and fluffy,
T eeth for eating.

Ellie-May Walker (6)
St Stephen's CE Primary School, Willington

My Puppy

P uppy,
U nder the blanket.
P retty,
P erfect pet,
Y ou can stroke him.

Tammy Clough (6)
St Stephen's CE Primary School, Willington

The Wolf

W onderful creature,
O n the mountain.
L ooks for food,
F luffy tail.

Riley Bell (5)
St Stephen's CE Primary School, Willington

A Crab

C rab lives in the sea,
R eally nippy,
A lways busy,
B ig claws.

Thomas Hodgson (5)
St Stephen's CE Primary School, Willington

Cat

C ool creature,
A t night they wander,
T hey have a long tail.

Jacob Wise (6)
St Stephen's CE Primary School, Willington

Cat

C ool creature,
A dorable fur,
T ickly whiskers.

Charley Westmorland (5)
St Stephen's CE Primary School, Willington

Lazy Panther

P athers are fast,
A s wild as a cheetah,
N ails are really sharp.
T heir fur is black as night,
H unt for animals to eat.
E yes as green as jade,
R oar as loud as a lion.

Carter Astbury (6)
St Vincent's Catholic Primary School, Penketh

Gorilla

G orillas are as black as night,
O n trees they climb,
R eally silly.
I t likes to eat leaves,
L ives with its family,
L oves its family,
A strong animal.

Louie Percival (6)
St Vincent's Catholic Primary School, Penketh

Jaguar

J ungle animals are scared of it,
A s fast as a plane.
G oes hunting in the night,
U ndercover it hides away.
A s black as coal,
R azor teeth as sharp as a sword.

Spencer Prockter (6)
St Vincent's Catholic Primary School, Penketh

Parrot

P erched on a tree in the jungle,
A nswers back.
R ainforest they live,
R ainforest they love.
O n the tree it hides,
T hey fly to find food.

Khiah Beard (7)
St Vincent's Catholic Primary School, Penketh

Monkey

M any bananas it eats,
O n the branch it swings.
N ever quiet,
K eeps bananas to itself.
E ating all the time,
Y ay for bananas.

Maria Henry (7)
St Vincent's Catholic Primary School, Penketh

The Animal Tiger

T igers eat meat every day,
I n the grass tigers hide.
G inormous tigers are big,
E at every day,
R est while waiting for their prey.

Georgia Halsall (7)
St Vincent's Catholic Primary School, Penketh

Good Koala

K oalas can climb up trees,
O n a branch.
A koala can climb fast up and down,
L ives in Australia,
A nd they go into the forest.

Noah Rigby (7)
St Vincent's Catholic Primary School, Penketh

Panda

P erfectly cute,
A s clumsy as a toddler,
N ever stops eating bamboo.
D oes not harm humans,
A jungle animal.

Phoenix Roberts (6)
St Vincent's Catholic Primary School, Penketh

Lion

L azy in the afternoon,
I ts teeth are as sharp as a knife.
O nly out at night,
N ever stops hunting.

Hani Biviji (6)
St Vincent's Catholic Primary School, Penketh

Scary Lion

L ions are soft as pillows,
I t only runs fast.
O h no, will he see me?
N ot friends with anyone.

Matej Kitanovski (6)
St Vincent's Catholic Primary School, Penketh

Bad Lion

L ion's teeth are as sharp as a sword,
I n the grass,
O n the grass it sleeps,
N ot nice.

William Partington (6)
St Vincent's Catholic Primary School, Penketh

Lazy Lion

L azy in the day,
I ncredible,
O bvious cat,
N ot nice.

Leo Clutton (6)
St Vincent's Catholic Primary School, Penketh

Unicorn

U nicorns are fluffy and also cute,
N o wolves like unicorns,
I n the forest is where unicorns live.
C olours on a unicorn are bright,
O nly unicorns are magical.
R eal people did not see a unicorn,
N o unicorns like tigers.

Daisy Morrow (6)
Stonehouse Primary School, Stonehouse

Flamingos

F lamingos eat upside down,
L ovely and pink,
A lgae is in water and flamingos eat it.
M arvellous creatures,
I n the water they stand,
N ot on two legs.
G ood at balancing,
O utside they live.

David Gray (6)
Stonehouse Primary School, Stonehouse

Penguins Are Nice

P enguins play games,
E ggs are for baby penguins,
N ice ice for penguins.
G ela the penguin had a baby,
U nder the water, penguins swim,
I nto the sea, they look for fish,
N aughty penguins like to play.

Elizabeth-May Ferguson (6)
Stonehouse Primary School, Stonehouse

Super Flamingos

F luffy,
L ovely,
A re very pink.
M any flamingos in the pond,
I nteresting creatures,
N ice and cute.
G olden beak,
O n one leg they can stand.

Halle Rodger (6)
Stonehouse Primary School, Stonehouse

Bunnies

B unnies can't eat a lot of carrots,
U nderground bunnies love to live.
N o bunnies are allowed out of homes,
N ice to play with bunnies,
Y ou have to look after a bunny.

Oliver Philbin (6)
Stonehouse Primary School, Stonehouse

Giraffe

G iraffes are cute and so lovely,
I nteresting animals.
R eaching high for leaves,
A nd they play a lot.
F ast runners,
F riendly,
E at leaves.

Lily Millar (6)
Stonehouse Primary School, Stonehouse

The Sun! They Are Dying

K oalas live in the treetops of Australia,
O nly live in one place in the world.
A ustralia has eucalyptus leaves,
L ovely creatures,
A mazing creatures need care!

Carly Davidson (6)
Stonehouse Primary School, Stonehouse

Cute Meerkats

M eerkats run really fast,
E at worms,
E at leaves.
R eceive food from Mum,
K eep a lookout,
A re cute,
T ime to pop out holes.

Finlay Steele (6)
Stonehouse Primary School, Stonehouse

Rhinos

R hinos eat grass,
H ave two horns,
I n Africa they live.
N aughty animals,
O utside running fast,
S o they like their baths in mud.

Rory Kerr (6)
Stonehouse Primary School, Stonehouse

Pandas Are Cute!

P anda babies are pink,
A panda only eats bamboo,
N asty animals are killing pandas.
D angerous animals kill pandas,
A panda is beautiful.

Lucy Bell (6)
Stonehouse Primary School, Stonehouse

Dogs

D ogs bite people and cats,
O h, dogs are fluffy and soft.
G o for a walk on the farm,
S ome dogs are bad.

Caylem Reynolds (6)
Stonehouse Primary School, Stonehouse

Dogs

D ogs are awesome,
O utside playing a lot.
G ood at chasing cats,
S itting cuddling up on the couch!

Millie Gardiner (6)
Stonehouse Primary School, Stonehouse

Dogs Are Awesome

D ogs are afraid of cats,
O ne dog barks at another.
G o for a walk,
S ome dogs growl at strangers.

Eva Cameron (6)
Stonehouse Primary School, Stonehouse

Cats Are Fun

C ats like to climb trees,
A re afraid of dogs.
T hey chase mice,
S ome cats have kittens.

Jamie Scott (6)
Stonehouse Primary School, Stonehouse

The Hare

H ares can jump higher than rabbits,
A re big,
R unning fast,
E xtremely good fighters.

Ross Gemmell (6)
Stonehouse Primary School, Stonehouse

Dogs

D ogs chase cats,
O h no, dogs bite cats' tails.
G reat pets,
S uper dogs.

Poppy Summers (6)
Stonehouse Primary School, Stonehouse

Wonderful Dogs

D ogs are cute,
O h, dogs play.
G reat pets,
S ome dogs like to play.

Caleb McVie (6)
Stonehouse Primary School, Stonehouse

T-Rex

T -rex is scary,
R eally huge,
E ats meat,
X -rays would be enormous.

Reece Cunningham (6)
Stonehouse Primary School, Stonehouse

Young Writers Information

We hope you have enjoyed reading this book – and that you will continue to in the coming years.

If you're a young writer who enjoys reading and creative writing, or the parent of an enthusiastic poet or story writer, do visit our website www.youngwriters.co.uk. Here you will find free competitions, workshops and games, as well as recommended reads, a poetry glossary and our blog. There's lots to keep budding writers motivated to write!

If you would like to order further copies of this book, or any of our other titles, then please give us a call or order via your online account.

Young Writers
Remus House
Coltsfoot Drive
Peterborough
PE2 9BF
(01733) 890066
info@youngwriters.co.uk

Join in the conversation!
Tips, news, giveaways and much more!

YoungWritersUK   @YoungWritersCW